Sanctuary Life

Reflections Of A Homeless Leader

By Shemekka Ebony

Copyright © 2023 Shemekka Ebony

The scanning, uploading, copying, or distribution of this book without permission from Author Shemekka Ebony is prohibited. For permission to use this book (other than for review purposes), please contact via email info@shemekkaebony.com. Thank you for honoring author's rights.

Published by © Shemekka Ebony

ISBN: 978-1-7371354-3-2

Thank You

I want to thank you for your interest in this book. If you are reading this, you or someone you know has identified you as a leader. It may be that through my lived experiences, you may find answers for yourself or a friend. This is a continuation of my While I'm Getting Naked journey of becoming more like the Church & Sanctuary. Reflections of my leadership transformation are captured within these pages. If you discovered Sanctuary Life before reading While I'm Getting Naked, please consider it a companion to this. Order your copy at www.WhileImGettingNaked.com

As mentioned in my previous book, there are so many angels in human form I met along the way that have influenced this book. For your curiosity, thank you. For your seed into fertile ground, thank you. If you gave your last dollar or minutes to get this moment to read along, thank you. Thank you for being a witness to our transformation. Yes, yours and my transformation to becoming brilliant leaders are here. May God bless you exceedingly as you grow comfortable getting naked about your lived experiences and learn to not feel as ashamed anymore while living with who you are in real life. Take time to journal while you read and find yourself becoming wiser while doing so.

I would like to thank God for my 'Hedges & Highways" calling that consistently saves my life! God is the brilliant source of my strength. Thank you, Michael Stewart-Isaacs, our Chief Daddy, and the Brilliant Bunch of children our love brings together. I would like to thank my elder sons, founders of Miles Missions; Lomari and Coren, who selflessly served on this missionary journey with me. Because our children are growing while watching, I am committed to keep walking out this call to lead.

Hello, interested reader, I wrote this for you. Thank you for accepting the invitation to examine your past and present while willfully welcoming transformation within yourself. If you are new to the While I'm Getting Naked Community, Welcome to our Space. Thank you for allowing me to show you how to discover your pathway to leading from within. I dedicate this book to any person who has ever wondered whether God called you to 'this'. You know what your 'this' is.

Foreword

I begin this epistle with the day the sanctuary doors were positioned open. Admittedly, God must often send me reminders about my call to walk by faith. I sometimes get impatient and want to rush along or assist God with alternate plans. On this particular day, my sons were sweeping the front of the church and had the doors propped open. I was busy trying to help God guide my life by filling out online job applications.

While I was busy helping God, God had an assignment for me. God sent Lisa to the steps of the church, and she asked my sons if she could speak to me. Lisa was a woman who seemed to be just walking along the highway. Lisa introduced herself and shared that she was called to walk across the United States spreading the gospel of Jesus Christ. She shared how God provides for her every need and how she is writing her book on walking by faith. At this point, I was speechless just listening to her share testimony after testimony of her hearing God's instruction and blindly following.

She shared how she trusts God daily, in every moment to cover her safety, make provision for food, and provide shelter for her and those individuals God assigns to travel along this faith journey with her. She shared how the fire station down the road told her to try the church at the blinking lights, after being denied several other places. For context, Hampstead, NC is a rural beach community. Our church was located along a main interstate highway. Well, our church doesn't have blinking lights on it, but it certainly had the doors wide open. I must note that the doors being propped open was a rare occurrence unless we were in service or transporting equipment.

She joyfully complimented the atmosphere as being warm and good. Lisa began to share how she had nowhere she felt safe to sleep for the night. Lisa was headed to Virginia walking from down south. I immediately offered her shelter in our church community center downstairs, affectionately called The Den. She seemed so grateful for the hospitality and stated that the previous night she slept in front of a locked church in Wilmington for safety. She said their front light was blown out, so she was safe and unseen till that morning. I shared some food, blankets, toiletries, and inspirational reading materials with Lisa for the night. I offered to assist her in sharing her story through our King Pen Publishing House for self-publishers and encouraged her to get rest. I texted some prayer partners of mine to pray for this traveling evangelist and asked for agreement for her healing of a cough she had. That night I came upstairs and prayed at the altar with my sons for her safe travels on her missionary journey. I was so struck by her arrival and knew she was sent from God to me. I shared thanks for allowing me to meet one of the angels encamped about me. I decided that this encounter with Lisa was connected to Sanctuary Life and must have been why I had stopped writing for a moment.

The next morning, I went down to The Den to thank Lisa for inspiring me and giving me her heartfelt testimony of walking by faith. In that conversation, Lisa reminded me of how God is always speaking to us, and how much God listens. I wanted to thank her for that. To my surprise, Lisa was gone. There was no trace of her ever being with us. The books I gave her were where I left them, as were the blankets. The only two things gone were Lisa and the church flier with my name written on it for when she was ready to move forward with her book publishing.

An encounter with an angel is far greater at the beginning of a book rather than at the end. Thank you, Lisa-wherever God has assigned, you. I hope you get this message, till we meet again. God bless Lisa and all other angels encamped around us on assignment to bring God's glory!

As you read along, I encourage you to also reflect on your own calling and leadership journey. You will notice nuggets you will want to highlight. Jot down your own 'aha' moments and life value gained while reading about my servant leadership journey.

Reflect On Your How You Define Servant Leadership

Servant leadership is a leadership philosophy that places the needs of others before one's own. It is a journey that requires constant reflection and growth. The first step on the servant leadership journey is to develop a deep understanding of oneself. This includes understanding one's strengths and weaknesses, as well as one's values and beliefs. Once one has a clear understanding of oneself, one can begin to develop a servant leadership mindset.

A servant leadership mindset is focused on serving others. It is a mindset that is willing to put the needs of others before one's own. It is a mindset that is open to feedback and criticism. And it is a mindset that is always looking for ways to improve.

The next step on the servant leadership journey is to develop a servant leadership practice. This includes finding ways to serve others in both small and large ways. It includes being willing to listen to others and help them solve their problems. And it includes being willing to stand up for what is right, even when it is unpopular.

The servant leadership journey is a lifelong journey. It is a journey that requires constant reflection and growth. But it is also a journey that is incredibly rewarding. Servant leadership is a way to make a difference in the world. It is a way to help others and make their lives better. And it is a way to live a truly meaningful life.

Table of Contents

1 Intro to Sanctuary Life — 8

2 The Call, The Engagement, The Marriage — 10

3 Life Without, Life Within — 14

4 Giving My Life to Christ — 17

5 Nothing to Lose, Everything to Lose — 20

6 Lay Aside Every Weight — 22

7 The Plagues — 24

8 Who Is Your DD? — 27

9 Life After Death — 29
    The Stripping
    The Soaking
    The Washing

10 The Doors of the Church Are Now Open — 34

About the Author — 36

Chapter 1

Intro to Sanctuary Life

I begin with this thought. Imagine, with me, a huge and established church facility. Imagine a church that stands out where it is planted and is seen as a leader serving many needs within the community. Now there is an interesting twist about this church, there are times in which it is closed, no services are held, and boards are put up to block exit and entry, much like when you are preparing for a hurricane or something. Can you imagine a church doing that? Closing for an undetermined amount of time out of nowhere? No one could have imagined that until a 'crown' pandemic arrived that closed all church doors. A church is usually the place in which the doors are often open and in times of really bad weather or crisis, is used as a shelter for others to come.

When I think of a sanctuary, I think of a place where people come to find God, feel His presence, find answers, and become healed. The church is where those that care about others come to get trained to better lead others within their families and communities towards the power to transform.

This writing is to tell you what happened when I decided to quit going to church. How do you wrap an introduction chapter to Sanctuary Life by saying I stopped going to church you might ask? It is because the more I stopped just 'going to church', the more I realized that I was becoming the church I needed and the Sanctuary I was seeking.

I AM THE CHURCH

The message of this book is to share with you my journey of giving my life to Servant Leadership and becoming the Sanctuary of the Church. The system labeled me homeless. The church labeled me a community pastor doing local missions. This book reflects the journey of discovery of how I learned to see myself in church and community. I support the church as a community sanctuary. It looks different for me. I don't go out of routine or out of familiar habits on Sundays anymore. I focus on my worship experience by having miraculous expectations and being ready to activate wherever I am. I still serve as a pastor sharing my gifts and relationship with God openly in my life. The difference is, I put being the church to practice every day I am alive, not just on Sundays.

No matter where the pandemic left your reality when it comes to being connected to a church. There is no better time than now, to revisit your calling and become the church your environment needs.

Reflection: Have you been called to lead? Are you a servant leader? How has your calling shaped you? Do you consider your calling as your life mission? Reflect on what you needed when you accepted your call while reading along.

Chapter 2

The Call, The Engagement, & The Marriage

The Call

For me to explain how I patterned my life after the church. I must first share how I first experienced my Hedges & Highways calling. One May evening in my 2012 apartment I shared with my sons, founders of Miles Missions, I heard my calling to missions. Here is how it happened. I was sorting through some items to donate. I heard a voice say, 'Forsake all and Follow Me'. I responded with a pious smile, yes Lord, I have done that. In reality, I had no idea the fullness of this request. I heard it again, 'Give it all up, and follow me'. I stood up, looked around, as if God was in the room standing nearby. I asked God, 'oh do you want me to give more stuff away?' In that moment, neon letters spelling the word MISSIONS flashed everywhere I looked. An overflow of thoughts to prepare for the mission field came over me. I knew about missions, from lived experiences in neighborhood missions, AmeriCorps VISTA, Intentional Living, Global Missions, and Church-based missions. (Into the Hedges and Highways of Communities was the assignment where I was being called to serve.) Through my calling, I better understood that everywhere my feet were planted were hedges and highways full of miracles, solutions, resources, and hope.

The interesting thing about this all is, I never question what I heard. I knew to be obedient and ready in my years of ministry experiences. I began getting rid of everything I possessed that I didn't need for my journey. I accepted the call, I said yes, all without considering the costs. I remember my pastor asking me over and over, Shemekka, are you sure 'this' is what you want to do? Are you sure you want to volunteer for this journey? He knew much more about what was ahead as he was a forerunner of his calling.

The Engagement

So, I released the following announcement about the engagement to our family and friends in May 2012:

We Are Engaged!! We have become One with the Body! (Ephesians 4:16) MSG

God is calling our family into full-time missions! We are seeking your prayers while we are in the field. God called us, presented the proposal for missions and our yes delivered our family's engagement in the Hampstead NC community. While in the field, the family will be available for ministry by traveling doing workshops, ministry assignments for gents dance ministry, or speaking, while in community development. I would love to present to any groups you feel led to invite us to. We are trusting God and freely giving back to his people what He has given to us. I'm favored by God to have the support of my pastor; the support of our Parent Partner, their dad, as well as God's first mission call, is located near one of the ministries that I'm a part of. I will be volunteering as Community Initiatives Director of Well Community Development Corporation as I serve as a grant writer and representative to our ministry's nonprofit organization. The gents are excited about it and ready to GO!

The Marriage

Now with all that enthusiasm, one could imagine a lovely journey, a clear-cut path, and all provisions ahead, right? It seems just right to think that way. However, it doesn't always go as planned. Let me explain. I came across a very nice riverfront rental home for our family located not far from the Hampstead location where we would be serving in ministry and community. The current tenants were projected to be out in June, and we would move in after that. Our previous lease was ending in June, so it worked out. I could store my items in Hampstead and spend some time camping out at the church until the property was vacant and ready. Note the use of the term camp out. See, this church was built in 1920 with a graveyard full of neighbors. This was no posh living arrangement.

July came and the owner said that the tenant needed just a little more time. I believed God for so much while camping out at the church. I was aggressively looking for grants that could serve the needs of this community, meeting with officials, and introducing our food resource initiatives to the community. I was also consumed a bit in the planning for a National Youth In Communion Faith Conference in New York, virtually from North Carolina.

While on the altar one day in prayer, I jotted down the words ***this is the fast I have for you***. The words 'be here, be present' flashed before me. I looked up the scripture that came to mind about God's fast for his people found in Isaiah 58:6-9:

"This is the kind of fast day I'm after to break the chains of injustice, get rid of exploitation in the workplace, free the oppressed, and cancel debts. What I'm interested in seeing you do is: share your food with the hungry, invite the homeless poor into your homes, put clothes on the shivering ill-clad, being available to your own families. Do this and the lights will turn on, and your lives will turn around at once. Your righteousness will pave your way. The God of Glory will secure your passage. Then when you pray, God will answer. You'll call out for help, and I'll say, 'Here I am.'

Yes, God. Who wouldn't want to commit to fulfilling this mission? As time went on, God revealed to me that His will was a season of living, saturating, and transforming in His presence at the church. While in New York, at the youth conference, I got a phone call from the homeowner of the Riverfront rental property. It's now August. I haven't heard from her in weeks and now she is urging me to get to the property with the deposit within the next day or forfeit the rights to rent. I am in New York, leading a youth conference, with no return plans for two more days. It was at that moment I had to imaginatively look 'my dream riverfront home/office' in the face and choose God's plan over mine.

In my leadership development journey, God often dealt with my options for me to take His ordered path. I could not believe that all the time from June to August, I was 15 minutes away from that beautiful riverfront property and could not get in it because it was occupied by someone else. I was told it was mine, she promised me first rights to it as soon as the tenant was out. Even after God told me what His will was, I still had a different desire in my heart. If you know me personally, then you already know I love being around bodies of water and nature. I would never have left that house; I would have always worked from home. I was ahead of my time in 2012 for remote work for sure. Hindsight 20/20, I'm so glad God showed me His way; it saved my life.

Reflection: Have you ever been led by God in a situation not supported by your people or environment? What was your situation? What leadership nuggets came out of that journey for you?

Chapter 3

Life Without, Life Within

A group of believers and church planters began this journey of sanctuary living all together in the church. That group got smaller over time as planters experienced the realities of living without comforts and dealing with people. Living with people that you don't know, that often are difficult to successfully work with, or don't have the same convictions as you, can be quite an adventure. I was the only mom who had their children living with them. I had a lot on the line with this faith walk and intentional living arrangement.

I remember sitting through meeting after meeting with staff/roommates figuring out ways to maximize the experience of sanctuary living and our ministry assignment. I look back and laugh now seeing that despite how many started, it consistently ended up being my children and I residing at the church. I know that was how God intended it to be anyway. It wasn't about getting through my call and engagement journey with a group of saints on a mission. it was about all of us *becoming* the will of God according to our readiness. It was less about their readiness and more about my understanding of their role in my transformation. I had to change my expectations that they too, were growing in the same areas at the same time as me.

Life Without

I titled this chapter 'life without' because one could easily look at our living commitment and assume my choice to live in a church with my sons is a charity case or my settling for underrated/unsatisfactory conditions. During our stay in the field, we went without the typical comforts we had when living on our own. Yes, we gave up having our own space, but we share our entire life, vulnerable in the presence of God in His House, the Church. We learned quickly to share everything. The kids learned to share their books and toys with church youth, and families in need, and pass through visitors with a cheerful heart. We learned that nothing belonged to us alone; it all belonged to God for His use. I remember weekends were somewhat challenging to get used to because many people would come to the church to hang out and much of our food resources would be eaten. I used to get so mad at being inconvenienced by others' inconsiderate nature of not asking before food was consumed. I reflect on those experiences and can see how selfish of me it was that my first response wasn't 'Thank you God that you bless me' to sow a seed (food) into someone else. I had to grow into having peace about it and declaring blessings over the food that was eaten. In my reflection, I realized that no matter how much of our food was eaten, I, nor my kids ever went hungry. These lessons taught me that as a leader, I had to ascend above my perceptions of scarcity and be more elated to share space and food that could be available to anyone who wanted it or was in need. After a while, there was personal space set aside for sanctuary residents, but thanks be unto God, I didn't need it. God delivered me from my immature self and sanctified those selfish imaginations and thoughts of scarcity that were stunting my growth.

Life Within

I title this life within reflecting on the things I thought I couldn't live without. Then God so lovingly revealed to me that I wasn't living life to the full. I wasn't living the way God intended faith leaders to live. I was living in a way of prioritizing getting my desires met that I somehow had made into my necessities. Don't get me wrong, God wills us to prosper and be in good health even as our soul prospers (Psalm 37:4). Can we look deeper? Are we prospering if we struggle to believe in God for what it takes to sustain the prosperity given to us? Are we being good stewards of our health if we are being gluttonous in our eating habits or storing up the food we won't eat before the expiration date arrives?

Let's pause for a quick activity! Let's head over to your food storage area and check your non-perishable food items. Go check your canned foods and boxed pasta for example. Have some items expired? I have found plenty of expired foods donated to the church food pantry to be redistributed to those hungry. People give things they don't want anymore and sometimes call it charity. If you could use those same resources that come through your hands and directly impact the lives of a community and ministry, would you?

Reflection Moment: My journey taught me what was necessary and what I can adapt to living without. It was because of the sacrifice of having my cell phone services cut off, that I began using free cellular service available through Wi-Fi and using Google Voice with other pilot phone applications at that time. I also learned the value of getting fresh food and produce from my community food bank to save on my resources. Life within began to mean living a more consecrated life. To think about it, why pay money for others to always have access to you no matter where you are or what you are doing? I'll be sharing much more about my life without/within throughout this reading. I can declare from experience that I didn't learn to live life on full until I learned how to live with less. There are so many things that I discovered about myself and my life when it was out of my power to have stable housing, cellular service, and transportation services to name a few. Some stories I share in this and others, you will have to hear in person at one of our live experiences.

Reflection: Reflect on the times in your life when you found yourself living outside of your comforts. How did that shape your leadership journey?

Chapter 4

Giving My Life to Christ

Many of us can think back to the time we felt the pull of salvation on our hearts and gave our lives to Christ. Others of us are unsure if we did the right thing, are waiting to get goosebumps, or one day before it's too late, we hope to accept Christ in our hearts and have evidence of some sort to prove it.

I have since learned that the thought of giving my life to Christ had a greater call attached to my assignment. For the most part, I thought I had done things right, I got saved, gave my life to Christ, lived holy, became a minister, then Elder, then Pastor Elect. Seems like a clear pathway to me. Then the question came to me, what does giving your life mean? Jesus gave his life while living and in death. With Jesus as a model, does my life reflect one given up for Him? Let's review, I wanted to go to college, and I went. I wanted to get married, have kids, and build a home and family, I did it. It wasn't until these things were mostly stripped from my grip that I realized that I was living my life, not the life God chose for me. My previous book *While I'm Getting Naked* introduces those testimonies and will help you understand my Sanctuary Life pre-work.

I served God in my life, but I hadn't given my life to God fully to use. I did what I felt was right. I even had moments of saying, "Wait, God, I'm doing too much in church", and "I feel I'm being used". I must laugh, thinking back at those times when I was going through development. (How can you feel like you are being used if you asked God to use you?) What I was experiencing was a bit of idolatry at work in my life. I made my happy life an idol and didn't consider what God wanted me to do with it. I filled my life with good works along with God's work and then was surprised when I got burned out. Can you relate?

Remember I mentioned parts of my life conveniences were stripped from me for me to understand the revelation of giving my life to Christ. Well, I had gotten quite comfortable with doing enough saved stuff to get by and go unnoticed because I had no spiritual accountability that trusted I could handle correction. I was a minister at a church, but I wasn't connected to a leader that could discern my spiritual gifts and mentor me. This time was around 2006, some serious events happened in my life that caused my ex-husband and me to be separated for 5 years. He was incarcerated, I was housing insecure, and our families were of no help to us financially. I was struggling badly trying to maintain our kids and marriage. I was presented with depression, anger, bitterness, regret, obesity, and several self-abusive behaviors. I welcomed the poor coping mechanisms to fill the voids of my stripping process. Feeling like I lost myself, I wandered in life day to day feeling disconnected. I certainly didn't want to remember what God said, because I stopped believing in my blessings being on the way for me. I was a functional, spiritual mess. Not understanding my message, forgetting there was hope, I wondered why there was no word from the Lord for me. Surely, with all this going on, someone will see my brokenness and minister to me. Nope, silence and deaf ears. Can you relate?

Those years were what seemed to be my hardest years going through what felt like a practical joke. When seeking help once, I remember being told by a retired pastor that I was going through a Job-like experience. After getting that word, I remember feeling like I'd rather have Job's boils and ignorant friends blaming me for my experience than go through my storm feeling strong and alone. Thankfully my ignorance and immaturity in spirit didn't disqualify me from God's grace to endure. Flashback to 2007, not many knew how bad things were for our family when my ex-husband was imprisoned. I was keeping a busy schedule ministering on Tuesdays, Wednesdays, and Sundays, selling cosmetics on days in between, and did I mention while working full-time at a Rape Crisis Center. God covered my whole development process. God's glory covered me so that I didn't look like the depression, anxiety, stress, bitterness, suicide ideations, and valleys I went through. God wanted me so much to find Him that He dealt with all my other options. No friends, no family, and no pastoral guidance walked me through that valley. I only had God, prayer, and devotionals. I remember going to a counselor once when my family unit was split apart. I remember that she looked at me and asked, 'How I was making it'? I laughed inside as she then told me about what didn't like about my situation and how her husband, also in law enforcement, was connected to it. That was the last visit. I could neither run nor hide from the call on my life and the development it was going to take for me to walk out my salvation and deliverance journey.

It was in these wandering years in my spiritual valley that God begin to condition my heart to feel comfort in Him. He conditioned my ear to hear His voice. I was still so guarded and untouchable, but the internal healing conditioning of my call to leadership had begun.

Reflection: Oftentimes leadership feels lonely and unattractive. I thought, why would someone volunteer for this? When you were called to servant leadership, what was your submission, obedience, and or surrender journey like?

Chapter 5

Nothing to Lose; Everything to Lose

Nothing to lose is a cliché we have become too familiar with when we feel like we have lost our purpose or direction. I remember feeling like I found myself Church HOPE'ing in search of a new direction. That's when I decided to move back to North Carolina from Virginia, closer to my children's father, who was still incarcerated, and running to a fresh start. This led to reconnecting with a ministry I partnered with during my high school and college years. The pastor was a childhood friend and spiritual leadership mentor.

God's voice of conviction and care came through reconnecting with a pastoral leader. God was showing me that being broken and bitter is no healthy place for anyone. Feeling like you have already lost is all is when God shows you how to use what's left. His ministry gave me messages of hope, feeling like a revival. Empowering words like *Lay Aside Every Weight* guided my weight loss journey. Messages like *God Loves A Stripper* guided me to come before God and take off the labels. *Who Do You Think You Are?* was a message that helped me heal while dealing with identity. *It Might Be Who I Was, But It Won't Be How I'm Known* demonstrated to me the freedom of serving God boldly, even with our shameful past. The list could go on.

This Nothing To Lose cliché was so far from the truth for me and was true. See, the truth was yes, I had to lose nothing because I needed to lose everything. And if I didn't hurry up and answer the call that saved my life, I could lose out on everything left that's important to God and me. I had to keep losing until I lost everything, lose the anger, lose the bitterness, lose the unforgiveness, lose the failed expectations, lose the bad choices, and lose the childhood memories of abuse. Now when I began to go after losing all of this, I began to lose physical weight without the assistance of exercise. I am a firm believer that, too often, our physical ailments are a physiological manifestation of psychological/spiritual challenges unaddressed. The more I let go of the harness of painful things, people, and memories, the less I found myself comforting my emotions with food and toxic behaviors.

Reflections:

Do you see connections in our life in which the memory of a painful experience overstays its welcome in your mind?

Did you overeat to comfort it? Did you harm your spirit/soul/body in other ways that you can identify?

If you answered yes to any of the above questions, All is well, and All is not lost. Keep Reading. Let me explain how you too can lose to gain.

Chapter 6

Lay Aside Every Weight

I'm reflecting on a time before living at the church that helped me center myself while transitioning from bitter to better in life. It was a September day after a mountain retreat when I saw a few candid shots, selfies, and some full-body shots of me that a friend of mine had taken. I could not believe what I was seeing. I was wearing 220 lbs. and I couldn't remember how I got there. I could no longer use 'baby fat' looking at my son who was then two. I didn't remember eating enough to gain that much, especially since stress had me down to 175 one year before that. It hit me; I had lost myself and was ready to find her again. I began to fast and seek God for direction. I was taking an herbal supplement that helped curb the cravings while I dealt with the spiritual cravings for change. What a difference effort made! I began journaling what I couldn't seek counsel about. With some coaching, I began detoxing bad habits to prepare for a long journey of healing. I found much more than I was ready for but was ready for change, nonetheless.

I also used this time to begin getting rid of stuff that I was holding on to mentally and physically. We naturally hold on to keepsakes that we feel quite nostalgic over. Some of us are extreme hoarders and others of us can't remember where anything of our past is. Wherever you are on the continuum, be considerate of this in the natural and concerning spiritual things. Are there some past relationships in which you still remember the anniversary date or keep in contact with the former significant other well beyond the break? Now is a good time to put all of that before the Lord and ask God to show you yourself and what you can let go.

Weight inconsistencies were my reality. I was struggling with the weight effects of PCOS (I was diagnosed in 2012 with the polycystic ovarian syndrome), a straining marriage, and raising two boys as a single parent alongside a husband co-parenting from prison. I had every excuse to sulk with depression in my spiritual valleys. Yet there was something inside of me that would let me settle any longer.

Reflection: How is your leadership showing up for you? Is your health being impacted by your unresolved worries? What are you going to do differently? Thinking like a leader means self-governance too. How can people follow you if you are unwilling to be naked with them at times? If a person can't see your grit to persevere, how can they be inspired to also lay aside the weights that are consistently holding them back?

Chapter 7

The Plagues

Let's return to the sanctuary season of my development in 2012. Being engaged in ministry was two-fold for me. It meant that I was preparing for my greater call as a Pastor in ministry as well as getting engaged in ministry more through my service in the community. Coming into this new commitment was a transforming experience to which I had to fully commit myself. I had to stand on what I knew God said to me while several things occurred to test my faithfulness to my calling. I call this part of the journey the 'Plagues'.

It was a time during my engagement and mission service in which all hell broke loose in some way in the natural and in my mind. It was my refiner's fire; the time when I had to ask myself whether I had heard God's call to missions in May 2012.

Going To Church

The first plague I encountered forced me to let go. God took the practical idea of downsizing to show me areas of my past I wasn't ready to let go. God took the practical idea of downsizing to show areas of my past that I wasn't ready to let go. I was going through items of my ex-husband that I boxed up and packed away. I hadn't had to deal with what was packed away. I was holding on not realizing that even though I filed the papers for divorce, I had not allowed God to heal all the disappointment of my failed marriage. I was determined to ensure we were cordial to one another for our sons. I even established that we would call each other 'parent partners' and not ex-husband & ex-wife. I didn't want to be identified by our failed marriage. I wanted to be known for our commitment to our children. It sounded good, but that declaration certainly had to be tried through the fire. Glory be unto God that we are both believers in

Christ; it helps us heal so that we could engage one another in our parental roles without bitterness or unforgiveness. I had no idea the residue of that pain was still there. In downsizing, I was able to find those things and deal with those emotions as they arose.

Living In the Church

The next plague came after I had settled in at the church. I had committed to what God said about living in the church when my son began to show a bad reaction to insect bites. It was the dog days of summer, and his skin sensitivity was literally taking the heat. He had flea bites on him from head to toe along with severe eczema flare-ups to boot. He would scratch the bites till he bled and had to wear socks to sleep in hopes of minimizing the scars. I remember crying at the altar wondering if my son was going to have to be placed with a relative while on this assignment, due to his little body being attacked so badly. The thought of not having my sons with me made tears flow like faucets on that altar floor.

God was silent during that time, and I had to keep serving. I remember being up late one night sulking at how bad this situation felt right now, and a call came into the church phone line. A woman began to share how she and her family had no food and were in great need. She had just arrived here in the area relocating from New Orleans and was not currently working. I told her that we could certainly assist her family and give them a ride to worship that upcoming Sunday if they desired. We delivered food and they came to the ministry soon after. They may have been grateful for the food, but I was grateful for the call. God answered by showing me why I was here. To take late-night calls, to provide a listening ear to a family in distress, and to make sure families have the necessary resources, which He had provided for me through this residency assignment.

Other plagues came to cause me to want to run, give up, and quit. From shaky church relationships getting worse to finding some of our clothes being destroyed by mice and mold. I was being tried on every side of my calling. But for everything I thought would destroy me, God showed me his glory. When relationships were destroyed, others were fortified even more. For the clothes I lost, I found God sowing new clothes into our lives. There is nothing that can replace the experience of feeling God be seen as a covering, a provider, a healer, and a deliverer when I chose to give my life to servant leadership.

No church plague proved hard enough to take me out. I know that was only the power of God raising me to be the sanctuary I was seeking to dwell in God's presence and not just visit there. Those that are the Sons of God must go beyond visiting the secret place (Psalm 91). The discipline just to dwell is hard at times but keep pressing for greater service in becoming the sanctuary and leader your community needs. Praise be unto God that He kept me during the plagues in our lives that were sent to destroy us. God has chosen me for greater accountability of service in becoming a Sanctuary in communities.

Reflection: God not only chose me, but God has called you as well. What has God called upon in your leadership development journey? How has your journey been? What plagues have been sent to distract or destroy you? What are you going to do about it?

Chapter 8

Who's Your DD?

Ok, so you have accepted the call, got engaged to your call, and survived the plagues that pushed forth your deliverance. Now what?

We must recognize the power of accountability when leading others in life, ministry, and career. It is important to have a spiritual DD or spiritual Designated Driver in our lives for accountability. Oppression weights can have you so punch drunk you can't trust yourself. Can you imagine dealing with spiritual strongholds which took years to grow and develop suddenly being willing to vacate your being without a fight? Not happening! It was much prayer, accountability, and God dealing with my options that brought on the change I needed to live. I remember that every time I'd isolate myself from others and attempt to fight my demons, imaginations, and emotions alone, I was never sure if I'd make it thru the night. If you have ever had night sweats or wrestled with your YES when no one else is around, find comfort in knowing this, too, shall pass! Having a spiritual DD in place helps lessen the burden of feeling alone.

It's, for this reason, I resolved that we all need a Designated Driver (accountability partner) that covers us while we walk through, strip free, and wash clean of the strongholds that gripped our lives. We need a DD to help us see what harnesses our growth and delays our development. As these strongholds and harnesses die, we can be born again out of the dust in God's image with a promise of new life. If we don't fill those voids with new life, the vacancy will welcome back the strongholds you once evicted.

There are those of us that have come through too much, have shown great progress, and still find ourselves struggling with a few areas in which we thought we were healed. We often think we are much further along in some areas of healing than we are. When we get touched in these areas that cause painful memories, we feel all we can do is run away. This is where your spiritual DD comes into practice. I ask my clients to identify patterns of running away from problems, "Where do they plan to go?". They usually share that they didn't have a runaway plan. I could identify with my clients' feelings to just get away and isolate. I also remember that those were times when God wouldn't allow me to be alone at all. I'd plan to go hide out at a friend's house only to find myself getting called to serve in some capacity. I'd shut my cell phone off, self-medicate, and try to sleep away the pain, only to discover that prescribed medications labeled may cause drowsiness, didn't work on me! I was able to share with clients those times when my desire to run would have me hiding out for comfort. The tactic of isolation is a self-destructive behavior to starve our spirit man. Separation is not the same as consecration. There is a difference between moments when God calls you into consecration to get into His presence and when we just wanted to separate from others at times, because we felt uncomfortable, tired, or frustrated with something or someone. Each situation is unique just as no two people are exactly alike.

I share this with you to express the value of a spiritually designated driver. In our spiritual life, a DD is a person that can sense when we need our ways of escape removed, and one who is a praying watchman (person on watch) guarding your vulnerable seasons of development. It may be a close friend or accountability partner. Whoever this person is, should be someone that can be activated to pray for you and guard your eye and ear gates until you are restored unto a sober mind.

Reflection: Who's your spiritual designated driver? How can you be this for someone else?

Chapter 9

Life After Death

To live is Christ, to die is gain (Phil 1:21). Each time we say no to our way, our will, our desire and die to our flesh, we have the opportunity to bring forth new life in Christ. Our sins, fears, past failures, our bitterness, jealousy, and bad attitudes must be put to death along with our childish ways. Our battles within to keep feeding those unhealthy areas cause them to grow and minimize our spiritual evolution of being a new creature. Every death brings forth new life. Get out of the grave! Don't stay stuck because it has become somewhere to hide.

Now, I must be nakedly transparent in screaming to you Dying to your flesh isn't sexy or cool in real life. Our old self must be destroyed. Anything that doesn't want to be removed will fight. One example of that is the truth behind why we are wearing masks. Our main reason is to hide from whom we wrestle within ourselves. We find ourselves dressing up our hurts, disappointments, and rejection. We tend to project that everything is well, yet within ourselves, we are dying to change who we are portraying. In our masks, we maintain our public posture to the public eye, but when we get alone, all of it pops up through our masks. Maintaining an 'I'm Ok' posture isn't the same as death to our flesh.

Jesus approached a man who was tormented by legion. The man's spirit spoke up before Jesus said a word. They asked not to be removed (Mark 5, Luke 8). Our strongholds do this to us too. It's in the form of justification, offense, reasoning, reaction, and the good ol' 'that's just how I am'. I offer you life now. Come out of the graveyard and receive your healing. Take off the masks of maintenance and walk in true deliverance. It may not be easy, but it is always worth it. My mentor always said, "Deliverance without discipline is deception." You no longer have to be deceived. Deliverance is a continual action, not a one-shot process. It takes many mistakes before we value true success. Be strong in the Lord and of Good Courage!

The Stripping

Taking off the masks builds character. I remember this stripping process. Some of it was voluntary, much of it not. I'm sure my journey will not identify with all, but much of this is for those of you that have a greater personal/spiritual call to a relationship and accountability to God. It's better described as the declaration of your YES to God getting introduced to your mandatory life changes. It's when your acceptance of the call bears fruit with seasoned roots. The more I was honest with myself and others about what I was walking through, struggling with, dying to, or coming out of, the more people would share with me that they needed to hear that. So, I began a quest of being naked and not ashamed of my servant leadership journey God called me to be on.

I learn to strip off the shame and seclusion of my struggles and make life with servant leadership more than the #Replay Sunday show. I began to transform my thoughts and confessions to be more in His image since I knew God called me to declare the gospel. As I matured on my journey, I understood this truth in theory and practice. I wanted others behind the cloth and those in leadership to know they have a voice of advocacy for what they can't disclose from the pulpit. I wanted others who felt that maintaining salvation was intangible or that it's a perfect life, to see the nakedness of a person that they admire also struggles to grow, fall, and be victorious.

That's why I am writing at this moment. I am writing to give a voice to those suffering in silence. As I strip, I understand the costs of being misunderstood, judged, or even condemned. It is for this victory I was created. Proverb 31 tells us not only to model a woman of virtue but to also advocate for those who cannot advocate for themselves. There is so much liberty in stripping the labels that are given to us or that we give ourselves while in an identity crisis. I have learned that I am not what I have been through, and I am who God says I am. I challenge you to make your list of things you desire to be stripped from you. Strip the things that bring pridefulness or shame. Let's strip ourselves from the immaturity of self-mutilating and self-seeking behaviors. Go ahead and strip from the painful memories of childhood abuse and neglect. Whatever you find hindering you or weighing you down, ask God how to begin your journey of stripping and for the courage to endure the process.

The Soaking

Now, we have begun the thought work of stripping, next, let me address the soaking. When we soak something, naturally we are trying to loosen some deep-down set-in stains that won't easily come out with washing. It's prep work with washing dishes, clothes, or even our bodies. Soaking softens hard stains. In the process, allowing ourselves to soak is a time when it may seem nothing is changing, yet so much is happening without our assistance. When you notice a soaking season upon you, you may want to incorporate a time of fasting, which would be like adding a detergent to the soaking water. God conditions us for what lies ahead as we are still in His presence. Things that are soaking are not busy being moved, they are still allowing cleaning agents to lift old things to rise to the surface. Some of your things will easily peel off on their own, while set in stains like past hurts, bad habits, and entanglements will need agitation like those found in the wash cycle to make it easier to clean. Allow those things to rise to the surface. It may be embarrassing to feel vulnerable in your soaking, but remember that those that don't understand you, wouldn't understand this anyway.

If we are not careful, our feelings may cause us to rush God's season of soaking. There is no time frame on how long your soaking may last or how often soaking will be required of you. Please remember this: Don't come out too soon, or you will need a repeat cycle.

The Washing

There's a song that says, 'Wash me over again; wash me over again, in that precious blood of the lamb....' This song makes me think how amazing it is to wash clean in God's presence. There are seasons ahead where your desire to be at peace in God's presence/worship will grow tired, cold, and/or stronger. Over time, asking God to wash us may turn into a routine and feel less powerful due to our busyness. When we are asking God to wash us, we are asking to be cleansed from all sin and unrighteousness. We need God to get all the areas, even our private places, the areas we are ashamed of or don't wash regularly when in a rush. It may seem ok to skip some areas during the washing, but in the long run, you will find dirt built up that will harden over time. Those skipped areas are much harder to fully clean later.

When God washes us, we are allowed to freely give all parts of ourselves for examination. There is nothing like being able to return to the manufacturer of our lives and destiny to be cleansed and upgraded to a vessel prepared for what lies ahead.

My sons' Saturday chore was washing the ministry vehicles in preparation for Sunday. Through modeling servant leadership, my sons serve in ministry with a cheerful heart on a day in which their peers are likely playing video games. Their heart isn't selfish to think that they can put it off for another time. We may treat our spiritual vehicles, or bodies as if we have time later to reset with a wash/rinse cycle. We can't treat our spiritual vehicles as such, otherwise, we work twice as hard to reset. We need regular maintenance just as the vehicles we drive daily.

The washing prepares us for whatever lies ahead and conditions us to take better care of our spirits between washes. I believe that if my sons can understand these principles now in their youth, they will be careful where they take their vehicles and what conditions they expose their spiritual vehicles to as they grow. We too, can learn from this. The truth is, you may not like the washing journey, but you are sure to love the look of the evident glow. Let your growth in God expand and evolve. Let God wash you often. Don't take too long between wash cycles. There is a nation of people awaiting your leadership to develop to guide them into their calling.

Reflection: When is the last time you had a stripping, soaking, or washing session with your creator? What can you easily identify in your soaking that falls off first? My soaking helps my attitude and judgments to be washed away and not become set in stains. When soaking, be prepared to find some hard stains that will need a little agitation (exploring in journaling) to loosen the hold and get to the origin (bottom of it).

Chapter 10

The Doors of the Church are Now Open

My call, engagement, and marriage to the church may be a little different than the average servant leader's lived experiences. I had to accept early that my journey is just that, mine. It does not mean I love God anymore or less than my co-laborers. It does mean that I have been chosen to walk a life in which my sanctuary is everyone's place of refuge, healing, strength, and empowerment just like the church. My engagement was a time of development, maturity, and sacrifice. I paralleled my life with that of a Bride being prepared to be married to the Church. I had to transform my ways, desires, and self-will to be able to effectively commune with God and the Church. I used to attend church with no thoughts of ever becoming more like the church. It wasn't on my radar or checklist.

What do your living epistles or writings say? What is written on the pages of your heart? To those of you that feel called to servant leadership, I challenge you to take the necessary steps in your life to become the sanctuary. You could be a part of redefining who Church Folk become after God calls us to serve in ministry and community. Be the one that chooses to heal and not hurt those coming to the sanctuary for assistance. This old hymn describes my preparation for Sanctuary Life so far:

> *Lord, prepare me to be a sanctuary Pure and holy, tried and true*
> *With thanksgiving, I'll be a living Sanctuary for You.*
> *It is you, Lord who came to save The heart and soul Of every man.*
> *It is you Lord Who knows my weakness,*
> *Who gives me strength, With thine own hand.*
> *Lord, prepare me to be a sanctuary Pure and holy, tried and true*
> *With thanksgiving, I'll be a living Sanctuary for You.*

Lead Me on Lord From temptation, Purify me From within.
Fill my heart with Your holy spirit, Take away all my sin.
Lord, prepare me to be a sanctuary Pure and holy, tried and true
With thanksgiving, I'll be a living Sanctuary for You.
(Author of song-Randy L. Scruggs)

This song originated many years ago and, in a moment, I experienced its hidden miraculous power to draw me into my sanctuary journey. I share this song with you to challenge you to reflect on the words during your self-evaluation. We may not all be called to live where we serve, but we all are called to be living epistles read my men daily (Read for yourself: 2 Cor 3:2).

The Doors of the Church Are Open. This sanctuary is a living sanctuary filled with thanksgiving, compassion, and love; all for God's pleasure. Let this living epistle meet you where you are on your journey. I celebrate and join you in ascending into your season of engagement after the call.

I would love to hear about your Becoming The Church journey. Journal your journey of becoming a better sanctuary and servant leader in your community.

About the Author

About My Daughter,

My daughter almost didn't make it. At 3 months, I almost lost her to a severe case of bronchitis. She had to spend two weeks in the hospital under a croupette tent to keep her alive and breathing, which she fought daily. I thank God, she made it, she was a special child then being prepared for the work she does now. Being a single parent, raising 3 children alone was not an easy task, I made sure they had what they needed and the sacrifice was worth it.

You're supposed to be the example for the child but I'm here to boldly say she is the best example for me once she got into high school. I wasn't ready for the way she was heading in God; I was running the other way. I started her out in church at an early age, the same way I was brought up. My mother took over when I didn't and for that I'm grateful. I'm thankful she didn't have to go through what I did, having to raise a family alone. I didn't do everything I should have but I did what I could.

I wouldn't trade her for anything. Her brothers were protective of her when they were younger even though she gave them a fit wanting to have it her way. I finally settled down once she made it through high school and found the place that I needed all along. I'm still striving daily, yet all I must do is look at her, and that keeps me going. Most of all, I thank God for being in my life and I can't make it without him. I totally depend on Him and being an independent person for years, I finally learned it wasn't me that sustained me but God with his awesome self. I am proud of who Shemekka has become.

-Evelyn Cannon, Mother of the Author Shemekka Ebony.

About the Author

Shemekka Ebony, Author of While I'm Getting Naked Journal Journey, is a Leadership Coach and Philanthropist who lives, works, prays, and plays with her husband Michael Stewart-Isaacs, their sons, Lomari, Coren, Chi-Alexander, and Ade'Maximus, and daughter Alihera in North Carolina. She holds a Bachelor of Arts Degree in Psychology and a Master of Science Degree in Counseling Studies and has co-authored serval research writings/publications addressing health equity, engagement tools, and engaging people with lived experience expertise. Much of this work was inspired by Shemekka Ebony's continuous lived experience journey in becoming the Sanctuary while in the hedges & highways. She has accepted her call as a Leadership Coach and shares the journey with her "Brilliant Bunch."

She is a passionate teacher, creative presenter, innovative leader, and self-proclaimed 'voice to the voiceless. She provides community and business engagement services in the forms of counseling, mentoring, leadership training, workshop/conference planning, and scheduling among many other talents and gifts. In her spare time, she loves the beach and writing. Shemekka Ebony and her family have dedicated their lives to igniting human connectedness worldwide by illuminating people's brilliance.

#IAmBrilliant #WhatMakesYouBrilliant?

Look for other inspiring and informative readings and research authored by Shemekka Ebony at Shemekka.com. Please feel free to reach her for booking and Leadership Coaching at www.ShemekkaEbony.Com

Scan the QR Code To Purchase More Writings & Gifts @ Shemekka Ebony's Online Store

Notes & Reflections

Trust In The Lord With All Your Heart.
Lean Not Unto Your Own Understanding.
Acknowledge God In ALL Your Ways.
God Will Direct Your Path.

www.ingramcontent.com/pod-product-compliance
Lightning Source LLC
Chambersburg PA
CBHW071324080526
44587CB00018B/3346